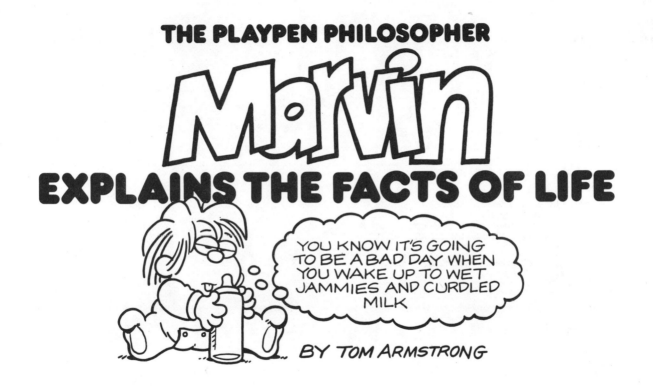

WORKMAN PUBLISHING, NEW YORK

For my family.

Library of Congress Cataloging in Publication Data

Armstrong, Tom, 1950-
    Marvin explains the facts of life.
    "The playpen philosopher."

    I. Title.
PN6728.M37A76   1983   741.5′973   83-16646
ISBN 0-89480-603-3 (pbk.)

Workman Publishing Company, Inc.
1 West 39th Street
New York, N.Y. 10018

Manufactured in the United States of America
First printing September 1983
   10   9   8   7   6   5   4   3   2   1

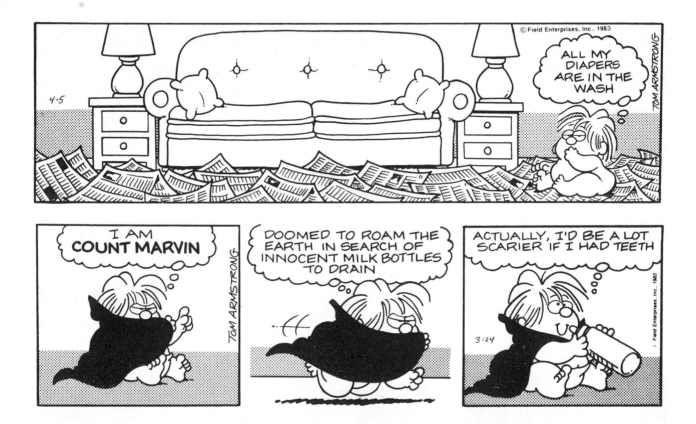

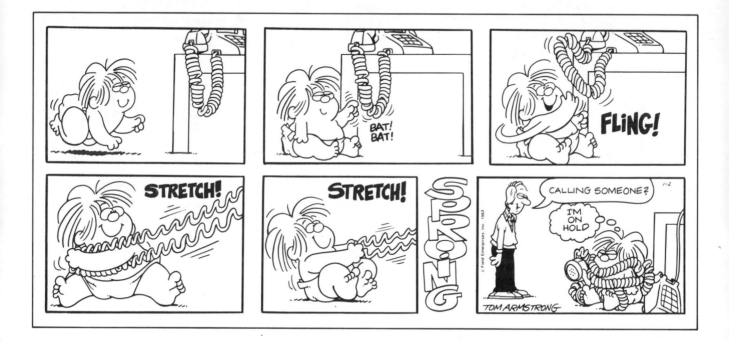

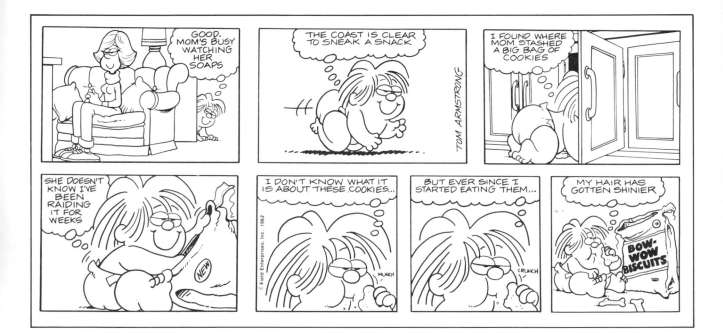

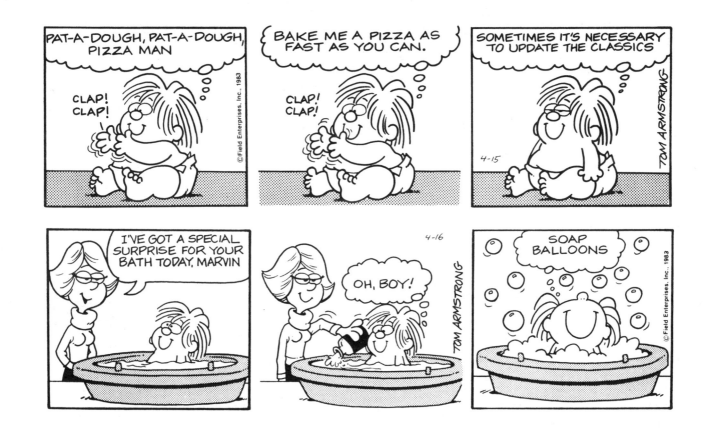